T5-AMD-105

to:

_____

from:

_____

Thank You Kindly

Illustrated by Becky Kelly

Written by Patrick Regan

**Andrews McMeel
Publishing**

Kansas City

04 05 06 07 08 EPB 10 9 8 7 6 5 4 3 2 1

ISBN: 0-7407-4704-5

www.beckykelly.com

Illustrations by Becky Kelly
Design by Stephanie R. Farley
Edited by Polly S. Blair
Production by Elizabeth Nuelle

Thank you
Carolyn and Laurie

Thank You Kindly

How can I begin to thank you
For the gifts you've given me . . .

For your friendship and your thoughtfulness,

Your caring words and deeds,

For all the times you've lent a hand

B. Kelly

Or a sympathetic ear,

And provided prudent counsel
When my thinking wasn't clear.

Thanks for listening to my secrets

And believing in my dreams,

And reminding me this old world's not
as crazy as it seems.

Thanks for bringing light into my life
On days the sun lay low . . .

For nurturing the best in me
And helping me to grow.

Thanks for making even uphill climbs
Seem like a pleasure ride.

I feel there's nothing we can't do
When we stand side by side.

Thanks for showing up and pitching in
When there was work to do!

The best of days are brighter still
when shared with friends like you.

I'm grateful too for quiet times

When words were left unsaid . . .

And wait with wide-eyed wonder
For the good times still ahead.

I don't know how to thank you
But I'll let this be a start . . .

And say thank you very kindly
From the bottom of my heart.